Original title:
Searching for Meaning in the Most Random Places

Copyright © 2025 Creative Arts Management OÜ
All rights reserved.

Author: Colin Leclair
ISBN HARDBACK: 978-1-80566-288-4
ISBN PAPERBACK: 978-1-80566-583-0

The Allure of Forgotten Doorways

Behind the old curtains, a sock lies lost,
It whispers tales of what it once tossed.
A mismatched shoe with a story to share,
Adventures forgotten, yet still filled with flair.

Under the couch, a sandwich awaits,
A relic of lunch, with uncertain fates.
Its crusts are like treasures, a bounty of crumbs,
Who knew such a find would invite so many hums?

In the attic, a hat, dizzy and round,
Claims to be a king from a time unbound.
With feathers and dust, it wears quite a grin,
Proclaiming itself the ruler of whim.

A mirror reflects what you can't quite see,
An echo of laughter, a spark of glee.
In corners forgotten, in creaks and old walls,
The quirkiest joy always loudly calls.

Glances at the Untouched

In a drawer full of spoons,
A rubber duck stands proud,
Mocking my every thought,
In this kitchen croud.

Amidst the mismatched socks,
I find a crumpled note,
It says, 'Eat the cupcakes!'
And wear your brightest coat.

A statue of a cat,
Winks at me with glee,
Is wisdom in the whiskers?
Or just lunacy?

The crumbs beneath the fridge,
Form hieroglyphs of bread,
Translating daily chaos,
With mayo on the spread.

The Echo of a Lost Sock

One lone sock on the floor,
It surely has a tale,
Of adventures in the dryer,
And the great lint trail.

It whispers through the dust,
Of fashions once so bold,
Did it dance with a shirt?
Or maybe just grow old?

The other sock is hiding,
In the depths of despair,
Conspiring with old towels,
In some laundry lair.

Yet still I search for answers,
In this cotton-clad quest,
For every sock discovered,
Is a fashion dream at best.

Finding Clarity in Chaos

Underneath the bed lies,
A kingdom of old stuff,
A tangle of lost treasures,
And socks not fit for fluff.

I opened up a box,
Filled with things I forgot,
A whoopee cushion reigns,
With a rubber chicken plot.

Among the crumpled papers,
And lost dreams in a jar,
I find a fortune cookie,
Its wisdom's rather bizarre.

The toys from days of yore,
Began to dance with glee,
In this whirlwind of nonsense,
I discovered silly me.

The Language of Unspoken Words

A chair with missing legs,
Holds secrets of the past,
It creaks a funny tune,
As memories are cast.

The cat stares out the window,
Dreaming up a grand thing,
While plotting all the squirrels,
With laughter as they swing.

A spoon and fork in love,
Embracing in a drawer,
Funny how they argue,
Yet need each other more.

In silence they all chatter,
Between the in and out,
Laughter buries shadows,
In the chaos, there's a route.

Treasures of the Lost and Found

In the corner, a sock awaits,
With a life story few can relate.
Keychains from trips long gone,
Friendships sealed with a rubbery prawn.

Here lies a watch stuck at three,
Time travel, perhaps, we'll see.
A spoon with a dent, a fork with a tale,
Hidden wonders, like a ship's sails.

Sentiments Sipped from Tea Leaves

Pour the hot brew, let thoughts collide,
A fortune teller with no guide.
Lemons dance, a honeybee laughs,
What's next, a horse or maybe giraffes?

A splash of sugar, a dash of spice,
Cups tell secrets, they're not too nice.
Watch out for bubbles, they might just pop,
Meaning's lurking, in every drop.

Comets in Cardboard Boxes

Shoeboxes stacked, a cosmic parade,
With glitter and doodles, a grand charade.
Old letters whisper, a postcard flees,
Wishes made on sticky notes, if you please.

Crayon rockets launch into the night,
A cat's meow, while the moon takes flight.
Inside the chaos, laughter and cheer,
The universe hides in each silly tear.

Revelations in Empty Cans

Guess what's hiding in a tin of beans?
Possibly dreams or medieval scenes.
A tomato's reign, a fish's last chat,
Discoveries thrive where we least expect that!

Pull the tab, unleash the lore,
Nothing's mundane when you open the door.
Each can, a portal to a world unplanned,
Where pickles wear hats and life's just grand.

A Prayer in a Parking Lot

In a sea of cars, I stand so lost,
Hoping one turns out to be worth the cost.
I ask the universe, 'Where's my ride?'
A pigeon coos back, with some reckless pride.

Oh, shopping carts laugh as they roll away,
Reminding me of my yesterday.
The light's red, but the laughter's green,
In this lot of dreams, absurd yet keen.

Chasing Raindrops on Tin Roofs

Tin roofs shimmer, a drumroll's song,
I start to dance, it can't be wrong.
With every drop, I stumble and sway,
Like a confused fish, I've lost my way.

Each puddle reflects my wild, frizzy hair,
While ducks quack gossip from over there.
A ballet of splashes, the ground laughs too,
Rain's just nature's way of saying boo!

The Wisdom of Shop Windows

Shop windows gleam with stories untold,
A mannequin points, looking regal and bold.
Dressed in fashion, but who's the true queen?
I ponder this with a face full of beans.

Sales signs shout with a confidence grand,
'Treat yourself!' but I can barely stand.
What's a good deal, what's lost and found?
In this bizarre bazaar, laughter's the sound.

A Forgotten Note on the Fridge

A note on the fridge, with scribbles and flair,
'Buy milk!' it declares, with a flair that's rare.
Beneath it, a magnet holding my dreams,
Or maybe it's just my leftover creams.

But what's this? A doodle of a dancing cat,
It silently judges my choice of hat.
In this chilly realm, thoughts slosh like soup,
The fridge hums a tune, of an awkward group.

The Art of Listening in a Noisy World

In a café full of chatter,
The barista spills a drink.
I nod like I've heard gold,
But I'm lost in a blink.

The couple nearby starts a fight,
As a dog steals a croissant.
I laugh, but I shouldn't,
What does that little pup want?

A train rattles by with might,
I tune in to the skies.
They whisper secrets of cats,
While I daydream of pies.

With earplugs in place,
I grin like a fool.
Sometimes the world just shouts,
But I hear it, that's cool!

Surprises in a Frayed Map

A map marked with coffee stains,
And a smudge from a snack.
I'm lost in the world's details,
With a banana in my pack.

Each corner holds a mystery,
Like socks without their mate.
What's hidden behind this tree?
A squirrel's a twist of fate.

I find a path to nowhere,
Covered in weeds and cheer.
With every turn I giggle,
This journey's full of weird.

The X marks where I stumbled,
But the prize is a good laugh.
For in a tangled journey,
It's fun that's the real map!

Patterns in the Clouds of Urban Life

Clouds gather like gossip,
In shapes of odd delight.
A rabbit? A pancake?
My friend spots a kite.

Buildings stretch to say hello,
With windows full of dreams.
I swear I heard a saxophone,
Or was it just my screams?

Pigeons march with purpose,
As if they own the street.
I look up for inspiration,
And find lunch on my feet.

Every shadow tells a story,
In a city full of jest.
The clouds laugh back at me,
In this lively urban fest!

The Beauty of Misplaced Keys

On the table, the keys tease,
Like they know I'm in a rush.
They dance around my mind,
    With a sly little hush.

Under cushions, they giggle,
While I search high and low.
I check the fridge for a snack,
But they're definitely a no-show.

In the fridge? No luck there,
Maybe they're on a spree.
Next to the cat in a sunbeam,
Oh, the trickery of these keys!

They were in my jacket pocket,
Fashionably late, I swear.
A laugh, a sigh, and then freedom,
Next time, I'll check with care!

In the Cracks of Pavement

Pavement cracks hold secrets deep,
A gum wrapper ancient, memories creep.
A lost penny dances in wet rain,
Wishes whispered, never in vain.

Each chipped tile sings a silly tune,
As pigeons strut, puffed like a balloon.
Sidewalk artists paint dreams so bright,
In laughter and chaos, we find our light.

Echoes of Forgotten Streets

Forgotten streets with stories bold,
Graffiti whispers of dreams untold.
A cat on a fence, surveying the show,
Plotting his escape from the world below.

Manhole covers, gateways to fright,
Old legends shared by a flickering light.
Each corner turned is a comedy scene,
Chasing dreams, unsure what they mean.

Serendipity Beneath the Stars

Underneath the sprawling night,
A pizza box claims it knows delight.
Stars giggle while the moon takes notes,
As lost socks sail on invisible boats.

Butterflies dance with a clumsy grace,
As laughter erupts in the strangest place.
Mismatched dreams float like kites in the air,
Profound thoughts on a sugary square.

The Geometry of Lost Keys

Keys scattered wide, a puzzling game,
Triangles and circles, who's to blame?
A sock drawer hides the best of fate,
In the shuffle of chaos, we celebrate.

With every clang of elusive metal,
Each snooze button hit feels like a kettle.
Chasing the lost, we find the absurd,
In the strange, sweet tunes of life, we're stirred.

Curiosities in a Jumbled Attic

Old hats stacked high, a musty smell,
A rubber duck peers, a forgotten yell.
Gran's sewing kit spins tales in threads,
While creepy dolls guard the sleep of the dead.

Dust bunnies dance on a vintage bike,
A broken clock whispers, but not what it might.
Paint cans chuckle at colors long gone,
As cobwebs weave stories till the break of dawn.

A map of nowhere hangs with a frown,
That leads to the laundry room, upside down.
Bottles of ink spill secrets untold,
While moths make poetry, both brave and bold.

In this treasure trove, we giggle and gawk,
What's this strange shape? A croissant or a rock?
In laughter we find the joy of the mess,
With each little find, we lovingly guess.

Reflections in a Puddle After Rain

A mirror of skies, but upside down,
Worms wiggle by, beneath glassy crowns.
Raindrops partner dance with dirt on the ground,
As puddles leak secrets with each tiny sound.

A duck waddle winks with a side of sass,
Chasing the clouds as they stumble and pass.
Socks splash gleefully, their owners complain,
Who knew joy thrived in each drop of disdain?

A paper boat sails on a whim and a hope,
Goes bumping along like a blushing old joke.
Parents seek children, lost in their play,
Made magical boats in the rain's brief ballet.

With each little ripple that dances in sight,
We laugh at the world as it drizzles with light.
As reflections remind us of whimsy's own game,
In laughter each splash, for it's all just the same.

Breadcrumbs on the Path to Nowhere

Tiny black crumbs mark a trail so bold,
Leading to nowhere, or so we are told.
A squirrel's gourmet feast, stolen small bites,
While giggles erupt from the tall, tangled sights.

In the middle of nowhere, we trip on a shoe,
Is it mine or your brother's? We've no further clue.
A hat on a tree makes a new fashion trend,
As the wind holds a party, no rules to amend.

Raccoons hold court near the tip of the path,
Judging our choices with soft little laughs.
With every wrong turn taken too fast,
The breadcrumbs remind of the fun that we've had.

So we wander, unpunctuated by plans,
Chasing our laughter with wiggly hands.
For in the absurd, we truly arrive,
Where breadcrumbs lead to the silly and alive.

The Poetry of Unopened Letters

Dusty envelopes stacked high on the desk,
Each one a riddle, a romantic grotesque.
What tales lie inside, we'll never quite see,
As they bloom like wildflowers, yearning to be.

Ink fades to whispers from the years that are lost,
To read them would surely come with a cost.
Friendships unfurl in the creases of time,
Wrapped in the scent of forgotten lime.

A love story messy, with stickers and stamps,
A time capsule garden where history clams.
Jokes laugh from paper, both crinkled and torn,
While thoughts in sepia are quietly born.

We giggle at fate, bold enough to conspire,
While unopened letters still spark our desire.
In the fun of the wait, the excitement resides,
What's written is safe, where the chaos abides.

Haikus at a Red Light

Cars honk, people stare,
Boredom's my best friend here.
A squirrel crossed my lane,
In my mind, he's the king.

Traffic lights are my muse,
Counting clouds, sipping blues.
A bird steals my fries,
Turns out, he's quite the guy.

Moments lost in thoughts,
Like socks from laundry knots.
Green light! Off we zoom,
Maybe next time, more room.

Echoes of Joy in the Unseen.

I found a lost shoe,
Just one, what's it to do?
Wonders of the street,
Invisible small feats.

A child's laugh drifts by,
On a breeze, it can fly.
Dancing on a whim,
No reason, just a hymn.

Umbrella flipped 'gainst wind,
A giggle might rescind.
Life's quirks bring delight,
In the chaos, take flight.

Whispers in the Wind

Leaves rustle, secrets tease,
A dance that's sure to please.
With each zephyr's breath,
I chuckle at what's left.

Bottles bobbing on waves,
Messages misbehave.
Where did that one go?
The ocean's inner show.

Grasshoppers play a tune,
Under a bright, full moon.
If you listen right close,
You'll hear the giggles boast.

Beneath the Unseen

Underneath the chaos,
A cat naps so leisurely.
Dreaming of sunlit beams,
Chasing invisible dreams.

An old bench starts to creak,
Sharing tales, oh so bleak.
But laughter's often found,
Where the odd thoughts abound.

Fountains burble with grace,
Tickling hearts in this place.
Life's odd twists unfold,
In laughter, it's retold.

Soliloquy from a Rusted Carousel

Round and round it goes again,
A horse with no name, what a pain!
It speaks of joy yet feels quite stale,
Where fortune fades, dreams turn pale.

The chime of laughter haunts the air,
As pigeons plot and watch my despair.
I whirl through time, missing my cue,
With cotton candy dreams that never grew.

A child's lost shoe hangs on the gate,
Whispers secrets of a forgotten fate.
I ponder fate beneath the stars,
Where luck and chaos form their bars.

And when I stop, a sigh escapes,
Echoed by nearby chicken scrapes.
On rusted metal, truths collide,
In carousel tales I've been a ride!

Revelations in a Dusty Bookstore

Amidst pages thick with irony,
I find romance, or was it sorcery?
A tome on squirrels, who knew they'd rave!
So many oddities, none to save.

The tales of wizards in mops and brooms,
And pirates hoarding kitchen spoons.
In this maze of paper, I roam free,
Where wisdom wears a musty tee!

A mystery novel in the self-help lane,
Promising me love but causing pain.
Do I need fortune or just a snack?
Here in this chaos, I lose track!

Each cover a door, each spine a guide,
In this endless dungeon where I reside.
I giggle at plots that seem so bizarre,
As I laugh with a ghost named 'Olde Tsar.'

Serendipity at the Checkout Counter

At aisle three, a cosmic dance,
I discover a stray chocolate romance.
A magazine beckons, 'become a star!'
While I wonder, should I buy that jar?

The line's a labyrinth of wants and needs,
Unleashing my greed like wild stampedes.
A rubber chicken in hand, I ponder,
Is this a purchase or simple blunder?

A grumpy toddler grins with glee,
While I contemplate the meaning of free.
The cash register hums a bizarre tune,
As I envision my life on a cartoon.

In this moment, the world feels light,
Surrounded by snacks, a joyous sight.
I pay my dues with squeaks and woofs,
In a wonderland of poorly drawn roofs!

The Secret Life of Lost Socks

Behind the dryer, a secret plot,
Where left socks dance and right ones plot.
They hold a ball every Wednesday night,
Swapping tales under a pale moonlight.

With mismatched guests from the laundry line,
A polka dot and striped, how divine!
They argue over whose turn it was,
To tumble in and lose their fuzz.

A missing mate strums a sad song,
Yearning to prove they still belong.
While lint bunnies serve gourmet snacks,
In the wild world where normal lacks.

And should you find a sock alone,
Remember the magic that it's known.
For when you look, and lose your way,
Socks write legends every day!

Soliloquy in a Coffee Cup

In the swirl of frothy foam,
I ponder life, my morning roam.
Could this latte know my dreams?
Or whisper secrets in its creams?

The barista laughs, he knows my game,
While I sip thoughts that feel quite lame.
With every gulp, I start to see,
Perhaps the world's absurdity.

Stirring sugar, I search for fate,
In this cup, I contemplate.
Who knew a brew could spark delight?
All my troubles, take a flight!

Espresso shots of whimsy cheer,
Caffeine dreams are drawing near.
Maybe here, in swirling steam,
I'll find my thread, or just a meme.

The Mystery of Abandoned Shoes

A single sneaker, dust collects,
With laces tied in perfect wrecks.
Who left their soles upon the street?
Was it a dance or quick retreat?

A partner lost, or shoes too tight?
They rest alone, what a sad sight!
Do they dream of running free?
Or plotting ways to flee from me?

A left foot musing on the right,
In mismatched tales of day and night.
Perhaps they're waiting for a pair,
To stroll the park or climb the stair.

Oh, curious kicks, so keen to roam,
Do you long for a cozy home?
While the world walks on, unmoved,
Your secret paths will stay unproved.

Secrets Beneath the Bridge

Underneath the arching stone,
I hear fish gossip, well alone.
Whispers float in rippling streams,
Of lost hats and soggy dreams.

Trolls doze off with books in hand,
While ducks speculate about the land.
What were they saying, oh so sly?
Maybe just, "We can't fly high!"

Old shoes draped on the railings sway,
Haunted by the joys of yesterday.
Passing trains sing their great refrain,
While the bridge stands firm in the rain.

Perhaps I'll take a little nap,
On history's lap, in nature's lap.
Under the bridge, life seems well,
With stories only water can tell.

Laughter in the Library

Among the books, I try to hide,
Yet giggles break my quiet pride.
A book on cats, it steals the show,
A feline author? Well, who knows!

Pages flipping, voices low,
But laughter bursts, just like a snow.
Histories laugh at gravity,
While science jokes at comedy.

Philosophy tosses a pun or two,
While Shakespeare winks, it feels so true.
In every nook, a chuckle found,
In dusty corners, joy unbound.

Books chat softly, whispers tease,
Reminding us to laugh with ease.
For in these walls of whispered lore,
We find the joy we can't ignore.

An Epiphany in the Garden

Amid the weeds and tangled vines,
A gnome with glasses reads fine lines.
He asks, 'Do daisies dream of sun?',
I chuckle, 'Only a little fun!'

The carrots whisper secrets low,
While ladybugs put on a show.
A shovel grins, I swear it does,
Digging deep for the next great buzz!

My hat's a little crooked, who cares?
With earthworms doing splits, who dares?
I trip on roots, my mind's a whirl,
In this wild patch, my thoughts unfurl.

To find a thought like it was gold,
Amongst the soil, so rich and bold.
With every weed I gently pluck,
I see the world, what priceless luck!

The Sound of a Distant Bell

A bell rings clear from way afar,
Is it a sign or just bizarre?
I follow sounds, it's quite a chase,
Past puddles and a rubber lace.

A cat's meow disturbs my quest,
Convinced its wisdom is the best.
'You'll find it where the kookaburras sing,'
But they just laugh, what a funny thing!

I spot a hat, all floppy and grand,
Is it the bell? Or a very strange band?
With every glance, the world feels new,
Flyers tap-dance, and birds say "Boo!"

The bell grows nearer, yet out of reach,
In this silly game, no lessons to teach.
But in this ruckus and charming sound,
I find myself, together with laughter around!

Fragments of a Soggy Page

A book alone in the rain does lay,
Its pages crinkled, in disarray.
I peel them back, a strange delight,
Full of thoughts that dance in sight.

A recipe calls for joy and whim,
But sugar's lost and salt is slim.
I laugh aloud at culinary dreams,
As puddles joke with sunlit beams.

Among the chaos, wisdom hides,
In every drop, a truth abides.
Laughter springs from lines gone rogue,
As umbrellas wear a rainbow vogue.

With every drip and soggy wit,
Heart peaks a little, it's quite a fit.
In wet reflections, the world appears,
Comic tales and playful cheers!

Discoveries in the Snow

A snowflake lands, it starts to jig,
In boots so big, my toes don't dig.
Frosty crystals whisper around,
In winter's grip, the laughter's found.

I build a snowman with a quirky grin,
He wears my hat, I let him win.
With buttons stolen from my coat,
He plays the tune of winter's note.

A squirrel scurries, quite the spright,
With tiny paws, it takes to flight.
It steals my berries for a feast,
While snowflakes join the frosty beast.

In this giggle-fest of chilly fun,
Every snowball's joke just can't be outdone.
With every giggle, I find a way,
To find the joy in this snowy play!

Synchronicity in Everyday Errands

In the aisle of the grocery store,
I find a shoe without its pair.
Is it lost or just on break?
I chuckle at its lonely stare.

The cart wheels squeak like a song,
As I dodge an old lady's glide.
We share a wink as we both throng,
Two errand pros on this wild ride.

Cereal boxes dance on shelves,
With cartoon mascots waving high.
I wonder if they dream themselves,
To escape this life as a pie.

At checkout, my total's a twist,
More than my wallet had planned.
The cashier comments, "That can't exist!"
"Just a magic trick of the brand!"

Musings on a Plastic Spoon

A plastic spoon rests in my hand,
Waiting for a bowl of glee.
It dreams of foreign lands,
But meets yogurt, oh so free.

What stories does it hold within?
Was it brave or just a waste?
Did it travel thick and thin,
For that moment, it was placed?

Stirring coffee, it finds delight,
Bouncing on the rim with flair.
Maybe soon it will take flight,
On a journey, it can share.

At last, it plops on kitchen ground,
Resigned to its humble duty.
Yet tonight, in sleep, it'll be found,
Riding waves of creamy beauty.

Breaths of Humor in Heartbreak

I tripped on love, a tough old shoe,
It laughed as I hit the ground.
My heart's a mix of black and blue,
Yet joy in chaos can be found.

A text arrived, my heart did freeze,
A meme of cats with ice cream,
In heartbreak's grip, I found some peace,
And lost myself in laughter's beam.

I wore my tears like a new coat,
Each drop a drip of comic flair.
With every sob, a chuckle wrote,
A laugh's the potion for despair.

So bring on heartache, it's a show,
With punchlines slung like love's dart.
I'll wear my humor, bright and low,
A wacky balm for a silly heart.

Delights Disguised as Mundane Moments

The toaster pops with joyful glee,
As I dance around my kitchen floor.
Breakfast for one, a solo spree,
With burnt edges, I still adore.

Laundry day, a sock parade,
Matchmaking on the kitchen chair.
A tumble dry turns love to fade,
Yet I'm the king of sock despair!

Water boiling, the kettle sings,
Like a diva warming up her voice.
Amid mundane, find curious things,
In every chore, I make my choice.

Even cleaning brings playful charms,
As dust bunnies race across my sight.
In every nook, laughter disarms,
Transforming grit into delight!

The Map of Forgotten Hopes

In a drawer full of socks, I found a clue,
A map marked with ketchup—it seemed quite askew.
It led to a garden with gnomes in disguise,
Where dreams sprout like weeds, chasing clouds in the skies.

Under the couch, a goldfish resides,
Winking at crumbs where ambition sometimes hides.
With a compass made of laughter, we wander the hall,
In search of the lost socks, it's a treasure for all.

A sandwich from lunch whispers tales of delight,
About pickles and mustard gone rogue in the night.
Rubber bands rescue paperclips from despair,
Crafting a jungle of wonders we never would share.

The pencil that doodles, believed dead and gone,
Sketches silly adventures until the dawn.
So here we cling tightly to moments so bright,
As the map of our hopes fades into the night.

Dandelions in Cracks

A dandelion sprouts from a crack in the stone,
It tickles the pavement, no longer alone.
With dreams in its fluff, it dances with glee,
Whispering secrets to wind: "Come play with me!"

The puddles are mirrors for frogs on parade,
In tuxedoed attire, they lean on the jade.
With each leap of joy, they croak out a cheer,
To remind us that life is absurdly sincere.

Between double lines on a street full of woes,
A message in bubbles, the universe glows.
With hope in their hearts, the weeds cast a spell,
In a world filled with chaos, they'll bloom very well.

So let's toast with our spoons to the dandelion's plight,
For in cracks of our journeys, they ignite our delight.
A laugh at the mundane, a wink at the day,
Finding gold in the dirt, come what may!

Afternoon Tea with Time

In a teacup of clouds, I brewed thoughts on a leaf,
Sugar cubes of laughter, a sprinkle of grief.
Time wore a hat made of whispers and zest,
One sip from the past felt like a curious quest.

The spoons did a slow dance, the forks joined the jam,
While biscuits debated if they were a scam.
Conversations were silly, like ducks in a row,
Each nibble a chapter, each sip stole the show.

The clock struck a 'meh' and rolled over in bed,
Counting sheep made of wishes that never were fed.
Who knew that the shadows would giggle and tease,
As the teapot spilled stories like autumn leaves?

So raise up your cup—the silliness swirls,
As the saucers conspire with giggles and twirls.
Here's to the moments where nonsense takes flight,
In the midst of our nonsense, we find our delight!

Echoes of the Oblivious Moon

In a wonky old chair under starlit design,
The moon wore a mask made of old tangerine.
Whistling sweet nothings to crickets and grass,
As if cluelessly judging all those who pass.

A shoelace's Twitter, a debate without pause,
On whether to tie or just cause a good cause.
The twilight chuckles, while owls roll their eyes,
At humans who dwell among mundane alibis.

A jellybean storm opened doors to the past,
Where memories twinkle like fireworks cast.
The moon, with its echoes, just hums and it sighs,
As laughter ricochets off the night's starry guise.

In this circus of wonders, we giggle and play,
With shadows as friends, we dance till the day.
So heed not the frowns of the tossers and glooms,
For the echo of joy breaks the silence of rooms.

Hues of a Broken Umbrella

In the corner of the street,
A rainbow lies, so bittersweet.
With ripped fabric, colors clash,
Each hue whispers tales of trash.

A child spins it, round and round,
Catching raindrops, joy unbound.
Forget the storms, the skies may pout,
This art piece reigns, no doubt, no doubt!

A dog sniffs it, thinks it's rare,
For treasures found, it doesn't care.
As puddles giggle, splashes fly,
Who knew the rain could kiss the sky?

In the wind, it dances free,
The humor's in our lunacy.
A broken thing, yet so alive,
In oddities, we learn to thrive.

The Rhythm of Broken Glass

On the sidewalk, shards do gleam,
Like tiny stars, they flash and beam.
With every step, a sound of crunch,
Making the world a lively munch.

The sweeping wind gives them a tune,
A symphony beneath the moon.
Each piece a note, the laughter flows,
Who knew that glass could sing, who knows?

Dance around those glittering bits,
A sudden twist, you might do splits.
With every slip, a giggle's born,
Adventures rise with every thorn.

So tiptoe through this sparkling maze,
Embrace the chaos, laugh in praise.
For life's a dance of joy and fall,
In pieces, we find our all in all.

Unexpected Truths in Coin Slots

At the diner, a slot machine waits,
Hoping for luck to open the gates.
Coins rattle, dreams do tumble,
In the chaos, we learn to stumble.

Each quarter tells a story bold,
Of chances taken, fate foretold.
But what's a win? A paper slip?
Or just the joy of the wild trip?

Fingers crossed for a cherry or bell,
Surrounded by laughter, what a swell!
With every spin, life takes a twist,
As fries are served, we can't resist.

The jukebox plays a goofy tune,
Under neon lights, we all are strewn.
Full of hopes, we cheer and boast,
In a coin's fate, we find the most.

Serenade of the Sidewalk

On the busy path, feet parade,
Each step a note in this charade.
With puddles reflecting silly grins,
And laughter soars as the day begins.

A skateboard zooms, a dog runs wild,
Sidewalk symphonies, laughter compiled.
The cracks in the pavement, nature's score,
Compose a ballad we all adore.

In the corner, a busker plays,
With quirky tunes, he brightens days.
Life's little quirks, a dance on the street,
In every odd moment, joy is complete.

So join the waltz, lose your cares,
In the serenade, everyone shares.
From the cluttered sidewalks, we're never apart,
Funny little moments, they warm the heart.

Whispers in the Wasteland

In the fridge, I found a sock,
Does it blend in with the clock?
Chasing echoes of last week's pie,
Why not dance with the pickle guy?

Beneath the couch, a lone shoe waits,
Pondering its past with the plates,
Was it lost in a grand parade?
Or just a victim of charade?

A paperclip beams under the light,
Dreaming of being a kite in flight,
Who knew junk had tales to share?
When life's a circus, do you dare?

Each cranny, nook, and forgotten space,
Holds a riddle, a curious case,
With a wink and a smile, I explore,
The weirdest stories behind every door.

Echoes of Forgotten Corners

There's a spoon that sings to the chair,
What secrets does it dare to share?
A dust bunny waves from afar,
Is it a traveler or a fallen star?

Old candy wrappers hold hands tight,
Whispering tales of wild delight,
Did they escape from the sweet shop?
Or are they just cruising for a mop?

A book with pages all out of whack,
Teaches me how to bring fun back,
In the closet, a garden gnome grins,
Challenging me to do silly spins.

Finding treasure where the shadows play,
Is where the laughter loves to stay,
In each corner, a giggle or two,
Proving randomness can be fun, who knew?

Fragments of Clarity in Chaos

In the chaos, I lost my phone,
Turns out it's chilling with a cone,
Ice cream laughs at my silly plight,
Could this be a sweet sign tonight?

A balloon stuck high in a tree,
Shrieks, "Come up and play with me!"
Are the squirrels hosting a dance?
I just might join, if given the chance.

Around the corner, a lost cat sighs,
Wearing a crown, it rules the skies,
Is it royalty or just a charade?
Whiskers twinkle like they're handmade.

Finding reason in the random fray,
Is the fun game I love to play,
With giggles echoing through the street,
Life's best moments are often sweet.

The Treasure Beneath the Cracked Sidewalk

A penny winks from the ground below,
Does it know where lost dreams go?
It holds stories of hopes, and wishes,
Of distant lands and fishy dishes.

Plants peek through cracks with a grin,
Sassy little greens, let the fun begin,
They giggle as they reach for the sun,
Talking smack 'bout who's workin' and who's done.

A pebble hums a tuneless song,
Claims it's been around all along,
With tales of frogs and their grand leap,
"Where's my spotlight?" it starts to weep.

In this world of astonishing find,
A little charm in the unrefined,
With laughter and cheer around each bend,
The quirkiest treasures never end.

Breaths of Old Book Pages

In dusty corners, tales reside,
A squirrel's waltz, a cat's wild pride.
Ink spills secrets, in quirky lines,
I find my thoughts among the pines.

A grumpy ghost in a leather chair,
Complaining why no one writes with care.
Characters dance on pages worn,
While I sip tea, a pulse reborn.

The plot twists like spaghetti strands,
And there's a dragon with rainbow bands.
I giggle soft at every quirk,
As time slips by, my heart at work.

Between the covers, laughter brews,
Finding gems in yesterday's news.
A bookmark holds my coffee stains,
Among these words, my joy remains.

This Feather is a Whisper

A curious feather floats through air,
Tickling thoughts that dance and dare.
It tells of birds who never flew,
And secrets known by morning dew.

A wink from clouds, a shout from bees,
I caught their chatter in the breeze.
This delicate brush makes me rethink,
Is this a feather, or just a wink?

I chase a fluff that wants to play,
Mimicking winds, it shimmies away.
With each quirky gust and playful spin,
I'm off on journeys where dreams begin.

Chasing whispers on a sunny day,
This feather dances, come what may.
In laughter's grasp, I lose my way,
Yet find more joy than words convey.

Captured Moments in Watercolors

A splash of blue, a dash of red,
My mind's a canvas, thoughts unsaid.
Sipping coffee with brushes poised,
Creating worlds where chaos is noise.

There's a rabbit wearing a hat so tall,
Telling secrets to the garden wall.
Each stroke a giggle, a fanciful jest,
In watercolor dreams, I'm always blessed.

The skies give way to marzipan pink,
As puddles chuckle and nightbirds wink.
I blend my laughter with joy's sweet sound,
On this canvas, I'm eternally bound.

Captured moments twirl and glide,
In joyous dances, I take my ride.
Colors collide, and I simply grin,
In this whimsical place, I eternally win.

The Soul of a Passing Train

A locomotive howls with glee,
Whisking memories, wild and free.
It rattles on with stories to share,
From clanging dreams to mismatched pairs.

As I wave to folks through the window's frame,
I wonder if they feel the same.
Stories of socks that went astray,
And a juggler's act gone hilariously gray.

The tracks laugh softly, like whispered tales,
Of bread loaves baked with jelly whales.
Each bump a joke, each turn a twist,
A circus ride that can't be missed.

I hop on board for the sights and sounds,
With clumsy dancers and quirky hounds.
In the soul of this train, I find my bliss,
With laughter echoing in every twist.

Rhythms in Ruined Attics

In the grumble of old boxes,
A sock puppet dreams of fame,
With dusty shadows dancing,
They forget their silly name.

A moth in last year's sweater,
Practices its tango stance,
While spiders write a letter,
To ask for one more chance.

The chandelier's a singer,
With icicles for backup tone,
Chasing dust bunnies around,
As if they're the Rolling Stones.

Stories in the old trunk,
Of buttons and of thread,
All the wishes fought and sunk,
In a world that's long since fled.

Enigmas Treasured in Silence

Underneath the old floorboards,
A raccoon hosts a debate,
On how to steal the world's cheese,
While the mice just contemplate.

The wall clocks tick in code,
Ticking things we never knew,
Are they counting all the seconds,
Or planning to take a zoo?

Cobbwebs write their memoirs,
And dustballs play charades,
Where puzzles aren't all puzzling,
And chaos serenades.

In the quiet little corner,
Of a room that seems so bland,
Riddles dance like silly dancers,
Leaving clues on every hand.

Wisdom Recovered in Silence

A goldfish whispers secrets,
Into the water's bright glow,
While houseplants roll their eyes,
At how slow the humans grow.

An old chair creaks in laughter,
Stretched out like it knows it all,
As it teases the wandering dust,
That dances with no recall.

The fridge buzzes like a prophet,
Hiding snacks of time indeed,
And the spatula answers back,
With spatters of wisdom freed.

Making sense of tangled wires,
The toaster aims to collude,
In the silence of the kitchen,
Where even bread can get rude.

Lapses Between Heartbeats

A cat contemplates the ceiling,
Wondering why it's so high,
To leap up for the goldfish dream,
Or just blink from a nearby lie.

A shoe sits pondering weather,
If it should run away,
While the carpet giggles softly,
In shades of green and gray.

Bricks confess their wise old tales,
Of stumbles and of glue,
While the paint peels off in laughter,
No one's feeling blue.

In the whispers of the twilight,
Between each heartbeat's call,
An echo of nonsense dances,
Just waiting for a fall.

Insights Beneath the Flickering Streetlight

Under the glow of a buzzing light,
I found a sock, oh what a sight!
It whispered secrets of a lost pair,
And made me question if life is fair.

A cat strutted by, with flair so grand,
Was it a king or just a stray band?
I asked about purpose, it gave a meow,
And dashed away like a fleeting vow.

A pair of shoes, mismatched and worn,
They told of adventures, both lively and torn.
Each scuff held laughter, each scratch a tale,
In this circus of life, I'm bound to bail.

With every flicker, new thoughts arise,
Through shadows and sidewalk, I search for the prize.
Perhaps it's silly, but here I stand,
With wisdom harvested from the lost and bland.

Conversations with an Abandoned Swing

An old swing creaked, beckoning a chat,
I took a seat, feeling quite fat.
It spoke of children, laughter, and flight,
How joy can vanish into the night.

It wobbled a bit, said, 'Don't take it hard,'
'Life's just a game, we're all playing cards!'
I giggled and swung, reaching for the sky,
Who knew deep thoughts could make you fly?

Leaves rustled softly, whispering low,
Each breeze a reminder of time's tricky flow.
"Is it too late to find something grand?"
Asked the swing, as it let go of the sand.

So I laughed with the swing, embraced its sway,
In this goofy chat, I found my way.
Home is where swings swing freely in glee,
Where wisdom arises from play and from me.

Finding Light in the Gloomy Alley

In a shadowy corner where the trash cans stacked,
I met an old rat, quite well-packed.
He twitched his whiskers, asked for a chat,
"Why so gloomy? Life's a welcome mat!"

He told me of crumbs in the depths of the dark,
Where secrets are kept, like a hidden park.
With pizza boxes and soda cans galore,
He claimed each find was worth searching for.

A puddle reflected the moon's wry grin,
While I pondered if hope could ever begin.
"Even rubbish can sparkle!" the rat proclaimed,
As I laughed at the wisdom he boldly framed.

So off I went, with trash-heap thoughts,
In every corner, my heart now caught.
For meaning can bubble, shine, and delight,
Even amidst alleys that bid you goodnight.

The Wisdom of Weathered Walls

I leaned on a wall, with peeling paint,
It sighed and told tales, quite quaint.
"Once I held secrets from lovebirds above,
Now I catch whispers of hope, and of glove."

Each crack was a story, each stain a song,
Of battles and feasts where I once belonged.
"Life's not just bricks, it's laughter and rain,"
The wall chuckled softly, easing my pain.

I found a no-parking sign, rusted and frail,
It claimed it once witnessed love's grand tale.
For every tag sprayed, a heartbeat anew,
"Here's to the moments, both silly and true!"

So I danced by the wall, its grace unconfined,
In a tapestry woven with life intertwined.
For wisdom's not hidden in books or in halls,
But stitched in the lives of our weathered walls.

Fragments of a Windowpane

In a café, I ponder cheese,
A mouse darted, took my sneeze.
The barista stared, eyebrows high,
But who needs sense when I have pie?

A dog on a bike, I laugh aloud,
Cycling past a bustling crowd.
He wags his tail, I spill my drink,
What does it mean? I pause and think.

A leaf floats down, with grace it sways,
I wonder how it spends its days.
It lands on bread—a snack divine,
Is the baker looking for a sign?

The sun dips low, a vibrant hue,
I spot a shoe, but not its crew.
Is there a lesson in lost attire?
Or just a life for shoes to aspire?

Wandering Thoughts on a Park Bench

An old man feeds the pigeons crumbs,
While squirrels dance, and laugh like chums.
I toss my thoughts to the skies,
Do birds know truths in their flies?

A kid on his bike, a treasure in tow,
A stick and a rock—what more do I know?
He gazes at clouds, I join his quest,
A flying whale? Just like the rest!

A ladybug strolls, with wings so bright,
She lands on my hand—a fine delight.
Do bugs share secrets as they roam?
Maybe they dream of a bigger home?

A toddler yells, "The sun is a cracker!"
Inspiring the birds with some lively clatter.
Perhaps the clouds wear whimsical hats,
Twirling and swirling, like acrobats!

Portraits of Dust and Shade

In my attic, cobwebs chat,
With dusty chairs, they plan a spat.
A broom walks in, all grumpy and mad,
Saying, "Enough, this slacking's bad!"

A sunbeam peeks, it breaks the gloom,
And suddenly shines on a broom.
"What are you doing?" the cobwebs snicker,
"Just trying to figure out my ticker!"

A forgotten sock meets a lone shoe,
"What's your purpose?" says one, feeling blue.
The sock replies, "To fluff when I'm tossed,"
"Together we're lost, together we're crossed."

In this corner, a dusty vase,
Wonders if it's found a grace.
But really, it just collects some specks,
Waiting for someone to cash in checks!

A Symphony of Crickets

At dusk, the crickets start their song,
Entwined with echoes, where I belong.
A firefly twirls, a disco ball,
Illuminating night's grand hall.

The moon winks bright, a sly old chap,
As I sit here, half in a nap.
My thoughts are tangled like spaghetti,
While crickets chirp, their tune is petty.

A frog nearby joins in the fray,
Croaking deeply, making the day.
Is it harmony or simple noise?
I can't tell, but I bring my poise.

As music swells from nature's stage,
I laugh out loud, I feel no age.
For in this chaos, I find my way,
In the random beats, it's all okay!

Lullabies from an Old Radio

A crackle hum, a distant tune,
Whispers float like a lazy balloon.
Dancing socks on the wooden floor,
Pajamas in tow, who could ask for more?

Beeping time, a cat's soft purr,
A toaster pops with a cheerful slur.
The old radio sings, forget the gloom,
Making magic from a tiny room.

Dreams Found in a Broken Glove

Underneath the couch, a treasure waits,
A glove that once held a mitten's fate.
Inside it hid a funky little dream,
A tiny car, a merry little team.

Squeaky toys, they bounce with glee,
Three-legged turtles, it's fun, you see?
Lost in the backyard, a world of cheer,
Imaginary friends always appear.

Secrets Left in a Park Bench

Wooden slats with stories to bare,
A secret love written with flair.
Sipped lemonade spills, a splashy scene,
Five lost shoes and a tangerine.

Squirrels gossip, a tiny squeak,
On the next bench, a dog dreams in meek.
Beneath the surface, laughter blends,
The park's alive, where the silliness never ends.

The Philosopher's Journal at a Food Truck

Churros and wisdom shared in a line,
'Is life just tacos wrapped up in thyme?'
Philosophers ponder with greasy hands,
Between bites, they sketch out their plans.

The ultimate question: where's my sauce?
Existential fries, what a glorious loss!
With every order, profound and bold,
Sipping syrup dreams, too tasty to hold.

Inquiries in a Cereal Box

I dug through flakes for wisdom rare,
But all I found was marshmallow flair.
The prizes hidden in corners tight,
Offered no clues in morning light.

I asked the spoon for life's best scoop,
It just laughed and joined the loop.
In each crunch, a quest begun,
But all I got was cereal fun.

The tiger winked, a promise made,
But all he gave was golden braid.
A prize of laughter, not a seam,
Still I pondered life's mad dream.

So here I sit with milk and cheer,
Hoping the answers might appear.
For in this bowl, my heart does bloom,
In silent giggles, I find my room.

Revelations at a Bus Stop

The bus was late, but time felt swift,
As pigeons gathered, sharing gifts.
One squawked loudly, wisdom he'd glean,
From old newspaper ads, he turned quite keen.

I met a cat in shades so neat,
He claimed to be the king of street.
With every tale of gutter fame,
I laughed and thought, 'Life's just a game!'

A lady beside me hummed a tune,
And claimed she danced with the lazy moon.
As we waited for our ride to come,
We found humor in trying to be glum.

So at the stop, beneath this sky,
I learned to laugh, to dream, to sigh.
With odd companions, hours flew by,
Bus or not, I learned to fly.

The Clock Ticks Triangular

In my room, time shaped quite odd,
It ticked in threes, as if it nod.
With hands that danced in a playful whir,
Each moment felt like a crazy stir.

I asked the clock why it turned that way,
It said, 'For giggles, not for play!'
I laughed aloud, what a nutty thought,
Life's humor is the best we've got.

Twelve triangles played tag on the wall,
Each angle laughed at my daily call.
With every strike and tock in place,
I joined the game, embracing the space.

So here in geometry's zany embrace,
I found a waltz, a light-footed grace.
With each tick-tock that came my way,
I danced to the rhythm of triangular play.

Conversations with Shadows

My shadow whispered secrets deep,
'Dance with me, let's never sleep!'
In twilight's glow, we shared our dreams,
Who knew shadows had such schemes?

It spoke of days, of glorious fun,
Of chasing light till the day is done.
We jived on sidewalks, in moonlit plots,
And bantered loudly, forgetting knots.

"Do trees ever talk?" I queried in glee,
"Only when folks forget to see!"
It chuckled low, a playful tease,
As we swayed with the night's soft breeze.

So in this dance of light and dark,
I learned my heart needs a little spark.
With my shadow, I found my place,
In laughter, life's a funny chase.

Reflections from a Rainy Day

Puddles on sidewalks, a mirror's grin,
Splashing reflections of the world we spin.
Umbrellas like mushrooms, all colors collide,
In this wet wonderland, our worries can hide.

Raindrops tap dance on the window pane,
Each one a note in a soft, sweet refrain.
Silly hats bobbing, a parade on the street,
Who knew losing an umbrella could feel so neat?

Raincoats and laughter, a whimsical sight,
Dancing in puddles, our hearts feel so light.
In the downpour, we find a rare bliss,
These playful disruptions we dare not dismiss.

So let the skies open, unleash their delight,
In the chaos of raindrops, we find pure insight.
In the laughter of strangers, the warmth of the spray,
We learn life's odd lessons on a rainy day.

Dreams Inside Dust Motes

Sunbeams streaming through the open door,
Dust motes swirling, like thoughts we ignore.
A sneeze brings giggles, a dance in the air,
Who knew our daydreams were lurking right there?

The couch is a cloud, the floor is the sea,
With every dust speck, imagination sets free.
We sail on a ship made of crumbs and old threads,
As dust bunnies plot from beneath the warm beds.

Chasing the sunlight like it's made of gold,
In corners and crevices, stories unfold.
Each moted soft whisper, a giggle, a sigh,
Is life just a joke? Oh, this dust might imply!

So grab your old broom, let the chaos convene,
In motes of lost dreams, our laughter is seen.
With a chuckle and shrug, let our thoughts all dance,
For life's oddest moments deserve a wild chance.

Light Play on a Broken Fence

The sun peeks through slats with a cheeky grin,
Creating shadows where the weeds have been.
A broken old fence, a canvas of time,
Where light plays hopscotch, a messily rhyme.

Butterflies frolic, they know all the tips,
In this rickety dance, no one takes trips.
Colors collide in old wood's embrace,
Each splinter a tale of a wild, wobbly race.

Cows munch nearby with a moo and a glance,
While fireflies twinkle, join in on the dance.
This patchwork of light, a whimsical sight,
In the brokenness shines the essence of bright.

So let's hang our dreams on the topmost nail,
In the jumbled up stories, let laughter prevail.
Through gaps in the fence where the sunlight bends,
We'll find silly moments that never quite end.

The Thread of a Stranger's Tale

In a coffee shop, a stranger spills tea,
While sharing their life, quite randomly.
Each sip of a story, a rush of delight,
With laughter that bounces, and froth in the light.

We stitch together moments from laughter and sighs,
As wild tales weave out through bold, curious eyes.
A fable of socks that escaped in the wash,
Who knew the mundane could make such a panache?

Lamenting lost keys and their sneaky retreat,
Each story adds flavor, life's odd little treat.
From wardrobe mishaps to dogs that wear hats,
We find wisdom in whispers of capricious chats.

So raise up your cup to the tales yet untold,
To the curious yarns that life weaves so bold.
In every small giggle, new journeys unveil,
We're all just bright threads in each stranger's tale.

In the Lattice of a Spider's Web

In a spider's loom, I took a glance,
Caught a tiny bug, in a wiggly dance.
With eight-legged grace, it spun its thread,
Whispering secrets, as it quietly said.

The dust bunnies giggle, a chorus of cheer,
Who knew that cobwebs held such good beer?
I raised my cup in a toast to the flies,
A toast to the webbing, with all of its ties.

Moths clapping wings, an odd night affair,
They tangled in laughter, knocked out the chair.
In the corners of chaos, wisdom takes flight,
Amid the oddities, I found pure delight.

So next time you stumble on fibers so frail,
Remember the spirits who danced in the pale.
They'll teach you that moments can twist and entwine,
In webs of the silly, we all can recline.

The Mystery of Abandoned Toys

In the attic's depths, old toys unite,
With tales of laughter and some tiny fright.
A doll with a wink and a car with a buzz,
Wondering where all their childhood friends was.

The teddy bears hold a council with pride,
Debating the blanket that sent them to hide.
A yo-yo and marble clash, oh what fun!
As they re-enact battles they've already won.

A robot in armor, rusted and gray,
Claims he's the king of this lost holiday.
With pranks and with jests, they fortify dreams,
In the glow of the dust, or so it seems.

So if you find toys that gaze with such glee,
Remember their laughter, from you they agree.
In their quiet rebellion, joy makes a stand,
For fun can be found in the oldest of bands.

Conversations in a Crowded Room

In a bustling room filled with chatter and cheer,
Muffin man mumbles, 'Have you seen my pier?'
While Sally discusses the price of her shoes,
Next to the cat with a very loud snooze.

A parrot joins in with a squawk and a flap,
Says, 'What's the gossip? I'm done with my nap!'
As glasses clink wildly, ideas take flight,
The stories weave magic past day into night.

Groucho and Cellophane laugh till they cry,
What's real, what's not? It's a strange lullaby.
Amidst all the winks and mysterious nods,
We find laughs in the chaos that not even gods.

So next time you wander through laughter and jest,
Remember the nonsense, and hang on with zest.
In the tangled connections, the real and the lame,
Life's funny in chaos, and fairy-tale fame.

Interludes Below the Stairs

Under the steps where shadows do play,
Lies a box of remnants from yesterday.
A lost sock, a marble, a fragment of love,
Whispering tales like a hand from above.

The mice hold a meeting, their tails in a flurry,
Arguing fiercely, creating a hurry.
While down under stairs, where the odd bits reside,
The sense of the silly is something to glide.

With a squeaky debate, turned into a show,
The dust bunnies dance with a little bit of glow.
They dream of the days when they roamed far and wide,
In a world of mischief, they happily bide.

So if you should wander and hear laughter near,
Don't be surprised at what you might hear.
For in the odd corners, life's humor can spawn,
Hidden delights that linger till dawn.

www.ingramcontent.com/pod-product-compliance
Lightning Source LLC
Chambersburg PA
CBHW071851160426
43209CB00003B/501